FOCUS ON

Grades 5-8

MIDDLE SCHOOL

ASTRONOMY

Teacher's Manual

Rebecca W. Keller, PhD

REAL SCIENCE 4 Kids

Illustrations: Rebecca W. Keller, PhD
                 Marjie Bassler

Focus On Middle School Astronomy Teacher's Manual
ISBN 978-1-936114-49-8

Published by Gravitas Publications, Inc.
www.gravitaspublications.com

Printed in United States

A Note From the Author

This curriculum is designed to give students both solid science information and hands-on experimentation. The middle school material is geared toward fifth through eighth grades, and much of the information in the text is very different from what is taught at this grade level in other textbooks. This is a *real* science textbook, so scientific terms are used throughout. It is not important at this time for students to master the terminology, but it *is* important that they be exposed to the real terms used to describe science.

For students, each chapter has two parts: a reading part in the *Focus On Middle School Astronomy Student Textbook* and an experimental part in the *Focus On Middle School Astronomy Laboratory Workbook*. In this teacher's manual, an estimate is given for the time needed to complete each chapter. It is not important that both the reading portion and the experimental portion be concluded in a single sitting. It may be better to have students do these on two separate days, depending on the interest level of the child and the energy level of the teacher. Also, questions not addressed in the *Teacher's Manual* may arise, and extra time may be required to investigate these questions before proceeding with the experimental section.

Each experiment is a *real* science experiment and not just a demonstration. They are designed to engage students in actual scientific investigation. The experiments are simple but are written the way real scientists actually perform experiments in the laboratory. With this foundation, it is my hope that students will eventually begin to think of their own experiments and test their own ideas scientifically.

Enjoy!

Rebecca W. Keller, PhD

How To Use This Manual

Each chapter in this *Focus On Middle School Astronomy Teacher's Manual* begins by providing additional information for the corresponding chapter in the *Focus On Middle School Astronomy Student Textbook*. This supplementary material is helpful when questions arise while students are reading the textbook. It is not necessary for students to learn this additional material since most of it is beyond the scope of this level. However, the teacher may find the information helpful when answering questions.

The second part of each chapter in the *Teacher's Manual* provides directions for the experiments in the *Laboratory Workbook* as well as answers to the questions asked in each experiment and review section. All of the experiments have been tested, but it is not unusual for an experiment to produce an unexpected outcome. Usually repeating an experiment helps both student and teacher see what might have occurred during the experimental process. Encourage the student to troubleshoot and investigate all possible outcomes. However, even repeating an experiment may not produce the expected outcome. **Do not worry if an experiment produces a different result.** Scientists don't always get the expected results when doing an experiment. The important thing is for students to learn about the scientific method and to make observations, think about what is taking place, and ask questions.

Getting Started

The experimentation process will be easiest if all the materials needed for the experiment are gathered together and made ready before beginning. It can be helpful to have a small shelf or cupboard or even a plastic bin dedicated to holding most of the necessary chemicals and equipment. The following Materials at a Glance chart lists all of the materials needed for each experiment. An additional chart lists the materials by type and quantity. A materials list is also provided at the beginning of each lesson.

Laboratory Safety

Most of these experiments use household items. Extra care should be taken while working with all materials in this series of experiments. The following are some general laboratory precautions that should be applied to the home laboratory:

▶ Never put things in your mouth without explicit instructions to do so. This means that food items should not be eaten unless tasting or eating is part of the experiment.

▶ Wear safety glasses while using glass objects or strong chemicals such as bleach.

▶ Wash hands before and after handling all chemicals.

▶ Use adult supervision while working with electricity and glassware, and while performing any step requiring a stove.

Materials at a Glance

Experiment 1	Experiment 2	Experiment 3	Experiment 4	Experiment 5

pencil
flashlight
	2 sticks (used for marking)
	2 rulers
	string
	protractor
	pencil
	square grid or graph paper
		basketball
		ping-pong ball
		flashlight
		empty toilet paper tube
		tape
		scissors
		a dark room
			modeling clay:
			  gray
			  white
			  brown
			  red
			butter knife or sculptor's knife
			ruler
				modeling clay:
				  gray
				  white
				  brown
				  red
				  blue
				  green
				  orange
				butter knife or sculptor's knife
				ruler

Experiment 6	Experiment 7	Experiment 8	Experiment 9	Experiment 10
the 8 planet models from Experiment 5 ruler (in centimeters) pencil large 1x1 meter (3x3 ft.) flat surface for drawing (can use cardboard or construction paper) large open space at least 10' long push pin piece of string a meter long	pen paper your imagination	pen paper computer and internet service Google Earth	pen paper computer and internet service Google Earth	pen paper computer and internet service Google Earth

Materials at a Glance
By type

Equipment	Materials	Locations

computer and internet service and Google Earth
flashlight
knife, butter or sculptor's
protractor
ruler in centimeters
rulers (2)
scissors
	Focus On Middle School Astronomy Laboratory Workbook
	basketball (1)
	modeling clay:
	    gray
	    white
	    brown
	    red
	    blue
	    green
	    orange
	paper, blank (several sheets)
	paper, square grid or graph (several sheets)
	pen
	pencil
	ping-pong ball (1)
	planet models (8) from Experiment 5
	push pin (1)
	sticks—used for marking (2)
	string (several meters)
	surface, flat—for drawing, 1x1 meter (3x3 ft.), can use cardboard or construction paper
	tape
	toilet paper tube, empty (1)
		room, dark
		space, large open, at least 10' long

Contents

Chapter 1: What Is Astronomy?

Time Required

    Text reading   30 minutes
    Experimental   1 hour

Materials

    pencil
    flashlight

Overall Objectives

This chapter will introduce students to the scientific discipline of astronomy. It begins with a brief history of astronomy and discusses how views of the cosmos have changed over time. Students should understand that the scientific discipline of astronomy began thousands of years ago and that modern astronomy utilizes the disciplines of chemistry *and physics to* study the universe.

1.1 Introduction

Astronomy comes from the Greek words *aster* which means "star" and *nomas* which means "to assign, distribute, or arrange."

Literally, astronomy means to assign, distribute, or arrange the stars.

Explore open inquiry with the following questions:

- *How would you arrange the stars?*

- *When you observe the stars, what do you see? Are they all the same size, shape, color?*

- *How easy is it to see the stars with your eyes?*

- *Can you observe any patterns in the stars?*

1.2 Early Astronomers

It is difficult to pin down the exact date when people began to observe the stars. Some ancient cave dwellings have primitive records showing human observations of the night sky from as early as 3500-3000 BC (BCE).

Many early civilizations used the positions of the Sun, Moon, and stars as a way to measure time and the changing seasons.

Stars can be observed anywhere in the world; however, constellations vary depending on the observer's location. Because the Earth is spherical, constellations seen from the northern hemisphere differ from constellations seen from the southern hemisphere.

Explore open inquiry with the following questions:

- *How might the constellations be different if the Earth were flat?*

- *If you were an early astronomer, how might you use the stars to measure time or the passing of seasons?*

- *Today, how often do people use the stars or the Moon to measure time?*

- *What other ways do modern people use to measure time?*

- *Which do you think is more accurate, modern timekeeping or ancient timekeeping? Why?*

1.3 Modern Astronomers

Advances in technology allow modern astronomers to look more closely at the celestial bodies seen by ancient astronomers and also to discover many more objects in space. Some of the tools that astronomers are now using will be discussed in more detail in Chapter 2.

It is important for the students to understand that astronomers rely on other scientific disciplines such as physics, chemistry, and mathematics to help them understand objects in space—how they move, how stars generate energy, what celestial bodies are made of, etc. Current scientific knowledge is based on a foundation of centuries of scientific thought and experimentation.

Explore open inquiry with the following questions:

- *How do you think math and physics help astronomers understand planets, stars, and solar systems?*

- *How does chemistry help astronomers understand how stars work?*

- *Do you think we could have landed on the Moon without math or physics?*

- *Do you think we might be able to fly to another solar system as we discover more math and physics? Why or why not?*

1.4 Changing Views of the Cosmos

One of the most important shifts in understanding happened when our view of the solar system shifted from geocentric (Earth-centered) to heliocentric (Sun-centered).

Changing such a viewpoint is a major contribution of scientific investigation. It is important for students to understand how this shift took place and the struggle that occurred between individuals with opposing viewpoints.

Explore open inquiry with the following questions:

- *If you were an early astronomer and did not have the tools of modern astronomy, what might be your observation about how the Earth, Sun, and Moon move with respect to each other?*

- *Do you think it would be easy to believe that the Earth is the center of the universe? Why or why not?*

- *Astronomers like Galileo had to convince others that observing the Sun or Moon moving in the sky was not proof that the Earth was the center. How hard do you think it is for people to change their ideas and trust new data?*

1.5 Summary

Discuss with the students the main points of this chapter.

- Astronomy is the field of science that studies celestial bodies. Remind students that a celestial body is any object in space, such as a planet or star.

- Review the activities of early astronomers and how they used the stars and movements of the planets to create calendars and to keep time.

- Discuss with the students how modern astronomy incorporates the disciplines of chemistry and physics to study the universe. Note that chemistry and physics are essential for understanding astronomy.

- Lead a discussion about how the entire way of viewing the world underwent a major shift when the idea of the geocentric cosmos was replaced by that of a heliocentric cosmos.

Experiment 1: Constellations   Date: _____

Objective   _____

_____

Hypothesis _____

_____

Materials

pencil
flashlight

Results

❶ In the evening on a clear night go outside and, without using a compass, locate "north." To do this you will need to find the Big Dipper. The Big Dipper is a set of stars that form the shape of a "dipping spoon." (The Big Dipper is not an official constellation but is called an asterism—a small group of stars.) The two stars on the end of the dipping spoon point to the star Polaris.

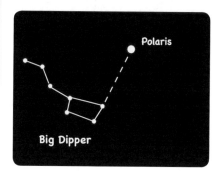

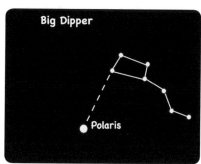

The goal of this experiment is to help students become familiar with the night sky, the stars, and several constellations.

This is an observational exercise, so there is no "Experiment" section

NOTE: This experiment is only applicable to locations in the northern hemisphere.

Polaris is the "North Star," and when you turn towards Polaris, you are pointing "north." It doesn't matter in which direction the Big Dipper is pointing, the two end stars always point to the North Star. The North Star is the only star in the sky that doesn't move (much). All of the constellations appear to move around the North Star. Once you find the North Star you can find nearby constellations.

❷ Now that you have found the North Star, try to find the constellation called the "Little Dipper."

Polaris forms the end of the handle of the Little Dipper.

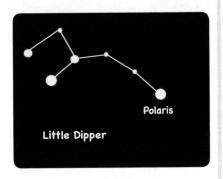

Draw the Little Dipper constellation as you observe it.

(Drawings may vary.)

❸ Try to locate the "Dragon." The Dragon constellation is between the Big Dipper and Little Dipper.

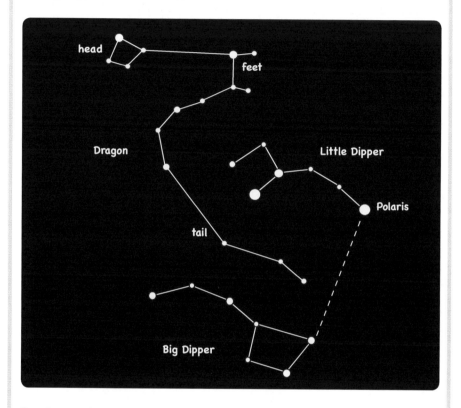

❹ On the following page, draw the Dragon constellation as you see it.

❺ Count the stars in the Dragon constellation in the image above. Compare this number with the number of stars you've recorded for the Dragon.

Draw the Dragon constellation as you observe it.

(Drawings may vary.)

❻ Record your physical location, city, state, or country, whether you are in the Northern or Southern Hemisphere, and the month.

Location _____

_____

Hemisphere _____

Month _____

Conclusions

Summarize how easy or difficult it was to find the North Star, the Big Dipper asterism, and the two constellations—the Little Dipper and the Dragon. What role, if any, does your physical location and the month you made these observations have on your results?

(Answers will vary.)

_____

_____

_____

_____

_____

_____

_____

_____

_____

_____

_____

_____

_____

_____

_____

_____

_____

_____

_____

_____

_____

_____

_____

_____

_____

Review

Answer the following:

(Answers may vary.)

▶ The word astronomy comes from the Greek word _____*aster*_____ which means _____*star*_____ and the Greek word _____*nomas*_____ which means _*to assign, distribute, or arrange*_.

▶ The word astronomy means _____*to assign or arrange the stars*_____.

▶ The word geocentric comes from the Greek word _____*geo*_____ which means _____*earth*_____ and the Greek word _____*kentron*_____ which means _____*point or center*_____.

▶ The word geocentric means _____*the Earth is the central point*_____.

▶ The word heliocentric comes from the Greek word _____*helios*_____ which means _____*sun*_____ and the Greek word _____*kentron*_____ which means _____*point or center*_____.

▶ The word heliocentric means _____*the Sun is the central point*_____.

▶ A constellation is _____*a group of stars that fit together to form a pattern*_____.

▶ The North Star is also called _____*Polaris*_____.

Chapter 2: Astronomers' Toolbox

Time Required

Text reading	30 minutes
Experimental	1 hour

Materials

two sticks (used for marking)
two rulers
string
protractor
pencil
square grid or graph paper

Overall Objectives

This chapter will introduce students to tools modern day astronomers use to study the stars, planets, our stellar neighbors, and the universe. Students should understand that one of the most important elements of scientific investigation is the use of proper tools for studying the world around us. Students should understand how modern technologies have shaped our understanding of the universe.

2.1 Introduction

Before technology began to play a role in astronomy, people used crude "tools" to study the sky. This section introduces students to the idea of "tools" in astronomy, such as the large stones at Stonehenge that helped early people mark the winter and summer solstices.

Explore open inquiry with the following questions:

- *Why do you think it was important for early people to mark the seasons?*

- *Without a calendar or a clock how would your daily life change?*

- *When early people were studying the sky, how do you think they were able to use the fact that the Moon and Sun move in a regular and predictable manner?*

- *How was the understanding of the cosmos limited by the lack of modern astronomy tools?*

2.2 Telescopes

Telescopes are an important tool used by astronomers for studying the stars and planets. Help students understand that a telescope aids the visualization of faraway objects.

The word telescope comes from the Greek prefix *tele-* which means "from afar" and *skopein* which means "see, watch, or view."

The history of the telescope begins with Hans Lippershey, a Dutch lens maker; however, Galileo was the first to make a telescope capable of visualizing the planets and their moons.

Explore open inquiry with the following questions:

- *Imagine how the telescope was invented. What might Galileo need to modify the Dutch "perspective lens"?*

- *Why do you think Galileo is credited with the invention of the telescope?*

- *What did Galileo need to know or understand to be able to modify the "perspective lens" to make a telescope?*

There are three main types of telescopes:

- Refractor telescopes

- Reflector telescopes

- Compound telescopes

The refractor telescope is the simplest type of telescope and has a straight, narrow tube housing a lens and eyepiece at opposite ends.

The focal point is the point at which the object being observed through the lens is in focus. The focal point varies with the shape and type of material used for the lens. The length between the lens and focal point is called the focal length. A narrow lens will create a longer focal length, and a rounder lens will create a shorter focal length.

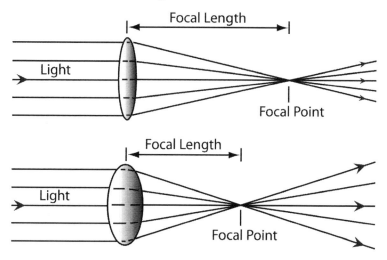

The magnification of a lens is proportional to the focal length:

M = focal length/focal length - distance of the object

Notice that as the distance of the object increases, the focal length must increase for the magnification to increase.

In order to overcome the limitations of refractor telescopes, reflector telescopes and compound telescopes use a combination of mirrors and lenses to focus the incoming light. This system allows for greater magnification for shorter focal lengths.

There are several different types of reflector telescopes of similar construction, including:

- Gregorian—introduced by James Gregory in 1663. The Gregorian uses a large concave mirror that reflects the incoming light to a smaller concave mirror that then focuses the light.

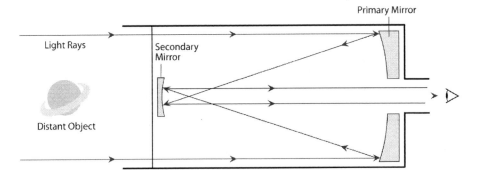

- Newtonian—introduced by Isaac Newton in 1668. The Newtonian utilizes one concave mirror and a flat secondary mirror to reflect the light to a focal plane at the top of the tube.

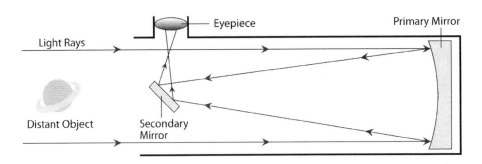

- Cassegrain—introduced by Laurent Cassegrain

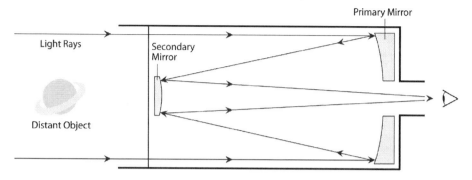

All three of these telescopes use some variation of lenses and mirrors to focus light.

2.3 Space Tools

One of the major obstacles to getting a good image of faraway celestial bodies is the turbulence created by the Earth's atmosphere. By attaching telescopes and computers to rockets and other probes that orbit Earth or travel beyond the Earth's atmosphere, astronomers can see the celestial bodies in space in more detail.

The Hubble Telescope orbits the Earth and is well above the distortions caused by the atmosphere. With the Hubble Telescope astronomers have been able to collect and report data in thousands of scientific papers.

2.4 Summary

Discuss the main points of this chapter with the students.

- Lead a discussion about the ways tools help astronomers explore the cosmos.

- Review the invention of telescopes and how the different types of telescopes work. Have a discussion about the astronomical discoveries that have been made possible by the use of telescopes.

- Discuss the tools that modern astronomers are now using to explore the cosmos. Help the students think about the ways in which having a variety of tools aids astronomers in the discovery of new facts about the universe.

Experiment 2: Measuring Distances   Date: _____

Objective   *To determine the distance of a faraway object using the method of triangulation (Answers may vary.)*

Hypothesis   *The distance of an object can be found using triangulation.*

(Answers may vary.)

Materials

two sticks (used for marking)
two rulers
string
protractor
pencil
square grid or graph paper

Experiment

In this experiment you will use a simple triangulation method to measure the distance of a faraway object.

❶ Find a wide open space with a distant object. The space can be a field, a city street, or even your own backyard.

❷ Pick two observation points, and place the sticks at these points. Mark one observation point "A" and the other "B."

❸ Take the two rulers and connect them at one end making a right angle.

❹ Place the corner of the double ruler on observation point "A" with one end pointing towards the object you want to measure and the other end pointing towards observation point "B."

❺ Attach the string to the stick at observation point "A," and stretch it out along the side of the double ruler pointing towards observation point "B." The string will be used as a guide so that you walk in a straight line.

❻ Holding the string, walk toe-to-toe from observation point "A" to observation point "B" making sure the string is still pointing at a 90 degree angle in the direction of point "B." Count your steps.

❼ When you get to point "B," attach the string to the stick. Check to make sure the string is still pointing in the same direction as the ruler.

❽ From observation point "B" find the object whose distance you want to measure. Place the protractor on the string so that you can measure the angle between point "B" and the distant object.

❾ Record the angle between point "B" and the distant object, and record the number of steps between point "A" and point "B."

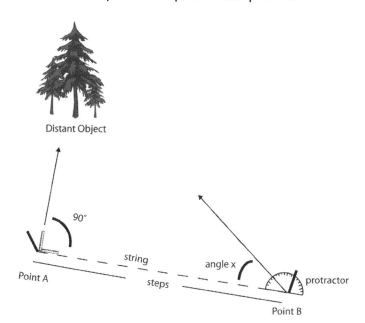

Results

❶ You will use graph paper and a modeling technique to measure the distance of the object.

❷ Take the square grid paper and mark point "A."

❸ Using one square for each step, find point "B" on the grid.

❹ Draw a line from point "A" to point "B." This is line AB.

❺ Draw a line from point "A" towards the distant object. This line should be at a 90 degree angle to line AB. Label this line "y."

❻ Using your protractor, make a line from point "B" to the distant object using the angle you measured. Extend this line until it intersects with line "y." (You may have to extend line "y" in order for the two lines to intersect.)

❼ Count the number of squares from point "A" along line "y" to the distant object.

❽ Assuming that each of your steps is .3 meter (one foot), how far away is the distant object? Record your answers below.

(Example—answers will vary.)

Number of steps—point A to point B   *19 steps*

Angle at point B   *45 degrees*

Number of squares—point A to distant object   *13 squares*

Distance of object in feet   *13 feet*

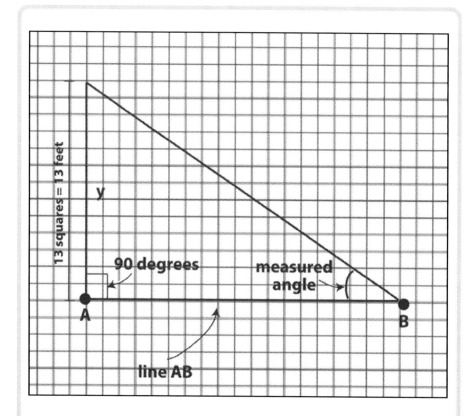

Example:

The graph should look something like this, although the actual distances and angles may vary. Make sure that point A has a 90 degree angle between line y and line AB. The students will use the protractor to measure angle B. Make sure the angle recorded on the graph is the same as the angle measured in Step ❾ of the Experiment section. You can help the students adjust the length of y as needed. Point out to the students that for smaller angles, y will be shorter and for larger angles, y will be longer.

Help the students discuss possible conclusions. Encourage discussion with the following questions:

- *How accurate do you think your measurement is?*

- *Could you use a different method to confirm your results? If so what would you do?*

- *What sources of error do you think might affect your result?*

Conclusions

Summarize how easy or difficult it was to measure the distance of a faraway object. Write down any problems or sources of error you might have noticed.

_____

_____

_____

_____

_____

_____

_____

_____

_____

_____

_____

_____

_____

_____

_____

Review

(Answers may vary.)

Answer the following:

▶ The three types of telescopes are:

reflector

refractor

compound

▶ The largest refracting telescope ever constructed was:

at the Great Paris exhibition in 1900

▶ Isaac Newton invented the _____*Newtonian*_____ telescope, which is a type of _____*reflector*_____ telescope.

▶ Atmospheric turbulence causes _____*particles in the air to move resulting in distortions in the optical measurements*_____

▶ List three types of spaceships that scientists use to explore space.

probes

landers

rovers

Chapter 3: Earth in Space

Time Required

Text reading	30 minutes
Experimental	1 hour

Materials

basketball
ping-pong ball
flashlight
empty toilet paper tube
tape
scissors
a dark room

Overall Objectives

This chapter will explore the Earth and its position in space. Students will learn about the effects of the Earth turning on a tilted axis and the effects of Earth's shape. Students will also learn how the Moon and Sun interact with Earth to create stability, weather, and tidal action. This chapter focuses on how the Earth is affected by the Moon and Sun. Chapter 4 will discuss the Moon and Sun in more detail.

3.1 Introduction

This short introduction stimulates inquiry with questions about the Earth. Help the students think about what they know about the Earth and its place in space.

Explore open inquiry with the following questions:

- *What is the shape of the Earth?*

- *Is the Earth round, flat, elliptical, shaped like a disk?*

- *How do you know?*

- *Is the Earth in the middle of the universe, off to one side, on the edge?*

3.2 The Earth in Space

The shape and size of the Earth and how it is oriented in space were topics of great interest to ancient people. Although there is some controversy about whether or not ancient civilizations believed that the Earth is flat, we know that some people believed this, and many were nervous about falling off the edge of the Earth if they sailed too far from shore. However, other people knew that the Earth was not flat, but round. Discuss with the students how it might have felt to have lived during ancient times.

Explore open inquiry with the following questions:

- *If you lived in ancient times would you think the Earth was flat or round?*

- *What evidence do you have that the Earth is round?*

- *What evidence do you have that the Earth is flat?*

- *How could you determine whether the Earth is flat or round?*

The word planet means "wanderer." Discuss with your students the meaning of the word planet and the criteria used to determine which celestial bodies are planets. Why does Earth qualify as a planet?

Many people think that the seasons are caused by the Earth's orbit around the Sun. However, seasons are caused by the tilt of the Earth's axis. Lead a discussion about the significance of having a tilted planet and how the tilt creates seasons. Also discuss with your students how the rotation of the Earth on its axis causes night and day.

> Explore open inquiry with the following questions
>
> - *Looking at the illustration of the Earth on page 17 of the Student Textbook, notice the tilt of Earth on its axis. How extreme do you think the seasons are at the poles? How extreme are the seasons at the equator?*
>
> - *How would life on Earth be different if the Earth did not have orbital obliquity?*
>
> - *Do you think the tilt of the Earth has always been the same?*
>
> - *What do you think would happen to living things if Earth was tilted on its side?*

3.3 The Earth and the Moon

Although the word for moon comes from the Greek word *menas* which means month, the word moon refers to any celestial body that orbits a planet. Note that not all moons orbit their planets monthly even though they are called "moons."

As the Moon rotates around the Earth, it is illuminated by the Sun at different angles. Because the Moon does not create its own light but reflects the Sun's light, we see different moon shapes as the Moon is illuminated from these different angles. We can divide the various shapes of the illuminated Moon into eight different phases:

1. New Moon

2. Waxing Crescent

3. First Quarter

4. Waxing Gibbous

5. Full Moon

6. Waning Gibbous

7. Last Quarter

8. Waning Crescent

Lead a discussion with the students about the appearance of the Moon being a result of the way the Sun reflects off the Moon's surface and that this changes as the Moon orbits Earth.

Exercise:

> Have the students observe the Moon, its size, shape, and color, and record their observations for a full month.

The Moon contributes to the creation of tides on Earth. The Moon, having a large enough mass, pulls on the Earth, and this pull causes the oceans to cycle back and forth between high and low tides. The location of high and low tides changes as the Moon orbits Earth, changing the direction of the pull.

Explore open inquiry with the following questions

- *If you did not know that the Moon reflected the Sun's light and that the Moon orbits Earth, what would you conclude about how the shape of the Moon changes?*

- *Do you think we would divide time in months if there were no Moon?*

- *How do you think the oceans would change if the Moon's orbit changed?*

- *What do you think would happen to Earth if the Moon was gone?*

3.4 The Earth and the Sun

The Sun also affects conditions on Earth. Although Chapter 4 will cover the Sun in more detail, it is important in this section to discuss how the Sun interacts with Earth.

The Sun provides energy for all life. On Earth, the Sun's light energy is converted to food energy through photosynthesis. Discuss how the Sun's energy is the source of fuel for all life.

Lead a discussion about how the Sun affects Earth's tides and weather. Sun storms cause disturbances in electric and magnetic fields that can have a profound effect on conditions on Earth.

3.5 Eclipses

An eclipse is a fascinating event to witness. When the Earth passes in between the Sun and Moon, a lunar eclipse occurs, and when the Moon passes between the Sun and Earth, we get a solar eclipse. Both types of eclipses can give us valuable information about the Earth, Moon, and Sun.

Discuss the two different types of eclipses with your students.

3.6 Summary

Discuss the main points of the chapter.

- A planet is defined as a celestial body that has enough mass to generate its own gravity, has cleared its orbit, and orbits a Sun. The Earth meets all of these criteria.

- The Earth's axis is tilted to one side rather than being parallel to the Sun. This tilt, called orbital obliquity, gives us seasons. The Earth also rotates around its axis once every 24 hours giving us day and night.

- The Moon is the celestial body that orbits Earth. The Moon's name is derived from the Greek word for month because our moon orbits the Earth about once every month. The length of time it takes other moons to orbit their planets varies.

- The Earth orbits the Sun. The Sun gives Earth the energy that is needed for food producing plants to grow and contributes to our seasonal weather patterns and tidal activity.

Experiment 3: Lunar and Solar Eclipses   Date: _____

Objective   *To examine the difference between lunar and solar eclipses*

(Answers may vary.)

Hypothesis   *The ping-pong ball must be in direct alignment with the*

flashlight to block the light falling on the basketball.

(Answers may vary.)

Materials

basketball
ping-pong ball
flashlight
empty toilet paper tube
tape
scissors
a dark room

Experiment

❶ In this experiment you will observe the difference between lunar and solar eclipses.

❷ In a dark room, place the basketball on top of one end of a toilet paper tube that is sitting upright on the floor. The toilet paper tube will hold the basketball in place.

❸ With the flashlight, walk several feet away from the basketball. Turn on the flashlight, and point it towards the basketball. While keeping the basketball illuminated, lay the flashlight on the floor.

❹ Holding the ping-pong ball, adjust it so that the ping-pong ball is between the flashlight and the illuminated basketball. Note the shadow that is cast on the basketball.

In this experiment students will use a basketball, ping-pong ball, and flashlight to model how lunar and solar eclipses occur. Have students read the experiment and determine what they think they will learn by doing this activity. Then have them fill in the *Objective* section.

Help the students write a hypothesis. Have the students think about what might or might not occur when they do the experiment. A possible hypothesis is given.

Students will need to place the basketball some distance away from an illuminated flashlight. The students will be holding the ping-pong ball and walking back and forth between the flashlight and basketball.

This exercise can also be performed by more than one student at a time, having the basketball, flashlight, and ping-pong ball each held by a student.

The point of the experiment is for the students to see how a shadow is cast by an object passing between either the Moon or the Earth and the Sun. It may take some time to find the location of the ping-pong ball that will result in a shadow falling on the basketball. Have the students note where they must place the ping-pong ball in respect to the flashlight in order to create a shadow. The ping-pong ball cannot be too high or too low, but needs to be in direct alignment with the flashlight.

❺ Move the ping-pong ball up until there is no shadow on the basketball.

❻ Now lower the ping-pong ball until there is no shadow on the basketball.

❼ Move the ping-pong ball in an "orbit" around the basketball. Observe where the ping-pong ball needs to be in order for the basketball to cast a shadow on the ping-pong ball.

❽ In the Results section, draw several of the "orbits" that you are testing, and note whether or not the ping-pong ball casts a shadow on the basketball or the basketball casts a shadow on the ping-pong ball (see the example below). You will need to spend some time "playing" with the ping-pong ball to observe where shadows occur.

Results

Example

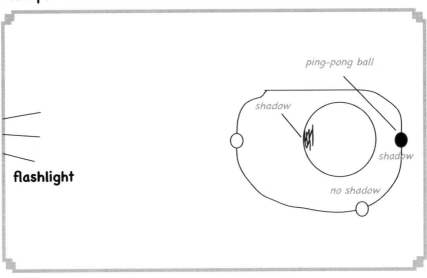

Conclusions

Based on your observations, discuss how a lunar eclipse occurs.

_____

_____

_____

_____

_____

_____

_____

_____

Based on your observations, explain how a solar eclipse occurs.

_____

_____

_____

_____

_____

Help the students write conclusions about what they observed. Have them note what happened if the ping-pong ball was out of alignment with the flashlight or basketball.

Review

Answer the following:
(Answers may vary.)

▸ The word planet comes from the Greek word _____*planetai*_____ which means _____*wanderer*_____.

▸ To qualify as a planet, a celestial body must meet the following criteria:

_____*orbit a sun*_____

_____*have its own gravity*_____

_____*have a cleared orbit*_____

_____*have a spherical shape*_____

▸ Define orbital obliquity and explain why this gives us seasons.

The tilt of the Earth's axis, 23 degrees from center

The seasons occur as the Earth tilts towards or away from the Sun

_____

_____

▸ The word moon comes from the Greek word _____*menas*_____ which means _____*month*_____. The Moon completes an orbit of the Earth every __*27*__ days.

▸ A lunar eclipse occurs when *the Earth passes between the Sun and Moon*

_____

▸ A solar eclipse occurs when *the Moon passes between the Sun and Earth*

_____

Chapter 4: The Moon and the Sun

Time Required

Text reading   30 minutes
Experimental   1 hour

Materials

Modeling clay in the following colors:
gray
white
brown
red
butter knife or sculptor's knife
ruler

Overall Objectives

This chapter will take a closer look at the Moon and the Sun. The focus of this chapter is to consider both the Moon and the Sun as celestial bodies and also to explore details not covered in Chapter 3.

4.1 Introduction

In this chapter we begin to move away from the Earth and the effects the Moon and the Sun have on it. We now take a look at the Moon and the Sun in greater detail.

Explore open inquiry with the following questions:

- *Explain how the Moon influences the Earth's rotation, weather, tides, and stability.*

- *Explain how the Sun influences the Earth's rotation, weather, tides, and stability.*

- *What do you think the Moon is made of?*

- *What do you think the Sun is made of?*

- *Do you think the Moon has an atmosphere like Earth's?*

- *Do you think you could live on the Sun? Why or why not?*

4.2 The Moon

In this section students learn about the features of the Moon. Our Moon orbits the Earth in a monthly cycle. In Chapter 3, students learned that the word moon comes from the Greek word *menas,* meaning month. Another term used to describe the Moon is "lunar." This term comes from the Latin word *luceo* which means "to shine bright." However, the Moon does not generate its own light like the Sun does. The Moon is made of rocks and minerals, just like Earth, and not gases like the Sun.

The Moon is smaller than Earth but is one of the largest moons in the solar system relative to the size of the planet it orbits. The Moon has no atmosphere, and because of this, temperatures on the Moon vary between both hot and cold extremes.

Explore open inquiry with the following questions:

- *How can the Moon be the brightest object in the night sky if it does not generate its own light?*

- *Explain how the smaller size of the Moon means that it has less gravity than Earth.*

- *Do you think the Moon has earthquakes? Why or why not?*

- *Do you think the Moon has storms or tornadoes? Why or why not?*

4.3 The Sun

The Sun, the Earth and the Moon are all celestial bodies. While the Earth and the Moon are composed of rocks and minerals, the Sun is a large ball of gas made almost entirely of hydrogen and helium. The Sun is many thousands of times more massive than Earth, with a radius of about 700,000 km (434,960 mi) compared to the Earth's diameter of 12,756 km (7926 mi).

The Sun rotates on its axis about once a month. As it is rotating, it spins faster at the equator and slower at the poles, with one rotation taking 25 days at the equator and up to 35 days at the poles.

The Sun contains no solid material and does not have a solid surface. The part of the Sun that we see when looking through a filtered telescope is called the photosphere, which is one of the outermost layers of the Sun.

The Earth's surface receives between 50 and 70 percent of the energy transmitted from the Sun to Earth. The rest is filtered out through our atmosphere.

Explore open inquiry with the following questions:

- *Do you think the Sun is much more massive than Earth? Why or why not?*

- *Do you think the Sun illuminates equally in all directions? Why or why not?*

- *What do you think life on Earth would be like if the Sun's energy output was more than it is now? Less that it is now?*

- *Why do you suppose that the gas that makes up the Sun doesn't just float away?*

4.4 Chemistry and Physics of Stars

The Sun and other stars generate energy in the form of heat and light by using thermonuclear fusion. Since the details of thermonuclear fusion are very complicated, all the student needs to understand at this point is that thermonuclear fusion occurs when two hydrogen atoms fuse at high temperatures and that the energy released from this kind of reaction is enormous.

To illustrate how much energy is given off during the thermonuclear fusion reaction of one gram of hydrogen, the students are instructed to consider the amount of energy in a chocolate chip cookie. The term "calorie" is used since it is an easily recognizable unit.

By definition, one calorie is the amount of energy needed to raise the temperature of one gram of water one degree. Energy units are also expressed in joules (J). One calorie equals 4.2 joules.

Explore open inquiry with the following questions:

- *What do you think will happen when or if the Sun runs out of hydrogen atoms?*

- *If the Sun were larger (or smaller) do you think the Sun would generate more (or less) energy?*

- *Do you think thermonuclear fusion would work with other atoms like chlorine or neon? Why or why not?*

4.5 Summary

Discuss the main points of this chapter with the students. Lead a discussion about the Moon being made of the same type of matter as Earth and how the Sun is made of different matter than both the Moon and the Earth. Discuss the different features of the Moon and the Sun.

Experiment 4: Modeling the Moon   Date: _____

Objective
_____

_____

Hypothesis
_____

_____

Materials

Modeling clay in the following colors:
- gray
- white
- brown
- red

butter knife or sculptor's knife

ruler

Experiment

❶ Model building is an important part of science. Models help scientists visualize how something might look in three dimensions.

❷ Observe the image of the Moon on page 27 of your student textbook. Note the colors of the core, mantle, and crust of the Moon.

❸ Using the modeling clay, build a model that resembles the image in your student textbook. Note any color variations on the surface, and try to duplicate the image with your model.

❹ Measure the diameter of your model Moon with a ruler.

Have the students write an objective for this experiment. Possible objectives are:

- *In this experiment we will explore features of the Moon by creating a clay model.*

- *Models play an important role in science, and we will use modeling to explore the Moon.*

- *We will use models to explore the three-dimensional nature of the Moon.*

Have the students write a hypothesis for this experiment. Possible hypotheses are:

- *By building a model of the Moon, we will get an idea of what the Moon looks like in 3-D.*

- *The Moon model will help us learn about the features of the Moon.*

Materials other than clay can be used to model the Moon, such as styrofoam balls or plaster of paris and paint.

Results

(Answers may vary.)

The real Moon is 3478.8 kilometers (2158 miles) in diameter. Compare the diameter of your model with the actual diameter of the Moon. Do the following steps to calculate how many times smaller your model is compared to the actual size of the Moon.

❶ Write the diameter of your model Moon in centimeters _____ or in inches _____*5 inches*_____. The diameter of the actual Moon is 3478.8 kilometers (2158 miles).

❷ Convert the diameter of your model Moon to kilometers.

If you are using inches, first multiply by 2.54 to get centimeters.

_____*5*_____ inches X 2.54 = _____*12.7*_____ centimeters.

Multiply the number of centimeters by 0.00001 to get kilometers. This will be a very small number.

_____*12.7*_____ centimeters X 0.00001 = _____*0.000127*_____ kilometers.

❸ Divide the actual diameter of the Moon by the diameter of your model Moon.

3478.8 kilometers (actual Moon) ÷ _____*0.000127*_____ kilometers (model Moon) = _____*27,392,125*_____

This should be a very large number. It tells you how many times larger the real Moon is compared to your model Moon.

Conclusions

How easy or difficult was it to build a model of the Moon?

_____

_____

_____

_____

_____

_____

_____

_____

Based on your calculation, how much larger is the actual Moon compared to your model Moon? What does this mean to you?

_____

_____

_____

_____

_____

_____

Review

Answer the following:

▶ The word lunar comes from the Latin word ___*luceo*___ which means ___*to shine bright*___ .

▶ Two types of rock that have been found on the Moon are:

___*basaltic*___

___*breccia*___

▶ Explain why the Moon has less gravity than Earth.

The mass of the Moon is smaller than that of the Earth. ~~Mass is~~ ~~proportional to gravity~~: more mass = more gravity; less mass = less gravity.

▶ The dark areas of the Moon are called ___*maria*___ meaning ___*seas*___ .

▶ The light areas of the Moon are called ___*terrae*___ meaning ___*lands*___ .

▶ Like Earth, the Moon has a ___*core*___ , ___*mantle*___ , and ___*crust*___ .

▶ Unlike Earth, the Moon has no ___*atmosphere*___ or ___*magnetic field*___ .

▶ The Sun is made mostly of two gases:

___*hydrogen*___ and ___*helium*___ .

▶ The Sun is about ___*100*___ times the diameter of Earth.

▶ The Sun generates energy through a process called ___*thermonuclear fusion*___ .

Chapter 5: Planets

Time Required

Text reading	30 minutes
Experimental	1 hour

Materials

Modeling clay in the following colors:

gray	blue
white	green
brown	orange
red	

butter knife or sculptor's knife
ruler

Overall Objectives

This chapter will take a closer look at the features of the eight planets of our solar system. Students will explore both rocky (terrestrial) planets like Earth and gaseous planets like Jupiter. Planetary orbits will be discussed in Chapter 6.

5.1 Introduction

In this chapter students explore the physical makeup of the planets in our solar system. Students will learn about the two distinct types of planets (terrestrial and Jovian) and the ways in which they are similar and how they differ.

Explore open inquiry with the following questions:

- *What is the Earth made of?*
- *What is the Moon made of?*
- *What is the Sun made of?*
- *How is the Sun different from the Moon and the Earth?*
- *What do you think Jupiter is made of?*
- *What do you think Saturn is made of?*

5.2 Types of Planets

In this section students will learn about the different types of planets. All of the planets are unique in some way, but there are also similarities. There are two major groups of planets—the terrestrial planets which are made of rock and the Jovian planets made of gas.

There are eight official planets—Mercury, Venus, Earth, Mars, Jupiter, Saturn, Uranus, and Neptune. Pluto is no longer classified as an official planet but rather as a plutoid or dwarf planet. Pluto is discussed in Section 5.5.

Explore open inquiry with the following questions:

- *What unique features do you think Earth has?*
- *Do you think Earth is similar to Mars? Why or why not?*
- *Do you think Earth is similar to Jupiter? Why or why not?*
- *What do you know about Jupiter, Saturn, or Uranus?*

5.3 Earth-like Planets

Mercury, Venus, Earth, and Mars are the four Earth-like (terrestrial) planets in our solar system. All of these planets are made of minerals and rock; all have rocky surfaces, craters, and volcanoes; all have similar densities.

Density is a measure of the compactness of matter, and since the four planets—Mercury, Venus, Earth, and Mars—have similar densities, scientists have determined that these four planets are Earth-like.

Although scientists have not traveled to these planets and can't measure density directly, they are able to estimate density by calculating the mass and volume of each planet using Newton's laws of motion and geometry. These calculations are beyond the scope of this text.

The following table shows the densities of the four Earth-like planets.[1]

Planet	Density (g/cm³)
Mercury	5.4
Venus	5.2
Earth	5.5
Mars	3.9

Explore open inquiry with the following questions:

- *Why do you think it is difficult for astronomers to get images of Mercury?*

- *What do you think the surface of Venus is like?*

- *Why do you think Mars has no liquid water?*

5.4 Jupiter-like Planets

The four Jupiter-like (Jovian) planets are Jupiter, Saturn, Uranus, and Neptune. Again, even though scientists have not traveled to these planets, they can tell that they are gaseous planets because of their density. The mass per unit volume (g/cm3) is much less for the Jovian planets than for the terrestrial planets. The formula g/cm3 means "grams per cubic centimeter" and is essentially "mass divided by volume," which is density.

[1]Reference: Astronomy Today, 7th Edition by Chaisson and McMillan, Addison-Wesley, 2011.

Following is a table showing the densities of the four Jupiter-like planets.[1]

Planet	Density (g/cm³)
Jupiter	1.3
Saturn	0.7
Uranus	1.3
Neptune	1.6

Explore open inquiry with the following questions:

- *Jupiter takes 12 years to orbit the Sun. How old would you be if you lived on Jupiter?*

- *Why do you think the rings of Saturn are made of ice?*

- *Why do you think Uranus and Neptune orbit the Sun so slowly?*

5.5 What Happened to Pluto?

Pluto was removed from planetary status by the International Astronomers Union (IAU) in 2006. Because Pluto does not appear to clear neighboring celestial bodies from its orbit, the IAU decided that Pluto does not meet all the criteria necessary for it to be called a planet. However, the planetary status of Pluto is still under discussion by astronomers, and Pluto may someday again be classified as a planet.

Explore open inquiry with the following questions:

- *Why do you think Pluto was considered a planet?*

- *Why do you think Pluto was demoted?*

- *Do you think Pluto will regain planetary status? Why or why not?*

[1]Reference: Astronomy Today, 7th Edition by Chaisson and McMillan, Addison-Wesley, 2011.

5.6 Summary

Review the summary statements with the students.

- There are officially eight planets in our solar system: Mercury, Venus, Earth, Mars, Jupiter, Saturn, Uranus, and Neptune.

- The terrestrial planets are "Earth-like" (made up mostly of rock) and are Mercury, Venus, Earth, and Mars.

- The Jovian planets are "Jupiter-like" (made up mostly of hydrogen and helium) and are Jupiter, Saturn, Uranus, and Neptune.

- Pluto was considered the "9th" planet in the solar system but lost its planetary status in 2006 and is now a considered to be a plutoid or dwarf planet.

This experiment focuses on model building. Model building is important in science and will help students learn more about the planets. The instructions given are for building models using clay, but other materials such as styrofoam and paint can be used.

Have the students write an objective for this experiment. Possible objectives are:

- *In this experiment we will explore features of the planets by creating clay models.*

- *Models play an important role in science, and we will use modeling to explore the planets.*

- *We will use models to explore the three-dimensional nature of the planets.*

Have the students write a hypothesis for this experiment. Possible hypotheses are:

- *By building models of the planets, we will get an idea of what the planets look like in 3-D.*

- *The models of the planets will help us learn about the features of the planets.*

Materials other than clay can be used to model the planets, such as styrofoam balls or plaster of paris and paint.

You may want to use additional references. Images of all the planets can be found at www.nasaimages.org

Experiment 5: Modeling the Planets   Date:_____

Objective

_____

_____

Hypothesis

_____

_____

Materials

Modeling clay in the following colors:
    gray
    white
    brown
    red
    blue
    green
    orange
butter knife or sculptor's knife
ruler

Experiment

❶ In this experiment you will model the eight planets of our solar system.

❷ Look closely at the images of the eight planets in Chapter 5 of your student textbook. Observe their relative sizes (which planets are larger or smaller than the others) and their shape and colors.

❸ In the following spaces write notes about what you can observe from the student textbook images. Also make a quick sketch of each planet, noting any important features, such as rings or spots. You will use these notes as a guide for your models.

(Answers will vary.)

Mercury

_____
_____
_____
_____

Venus

_____
_____
_____
_____

Earth

_____
_____
_____
_____

Mars

_____
_____
_____
_____

Jupiter

_____

_____

_____

_____

Saturn

_____

_____

_____

_____

Uranus

_____

_____

_____

_____

Neptune

_____

_____

_____

_____

❹ Using the modeling clay, create a model of each planet. Make sure that you keep the relative sizes in proportion (Jupiter is larger than Earth, Mercury is smaller than Venus, and so on).

Results

Observe the model planets you have created. Are they the correct relative size? Do they match the images in the book? Are they all spherical in shape? Record your observations below:

_____

_____

_____

_____

_____

_____

_____

_____

_____

_____

_____

_____

_____

_____

_____

_____

Conclusions

How easy or difficult was it to build the models of the planets?

_____

_____

_____

_____

_____

_____

_____

_____

Discuss how well your models do or do not represent the real planets.

_____

_____

_____

_____

_____

_____

Review

Answer the following:

▶ List the eight planets of the solar system, from closest to farthest from the Sun.

> *Mercury*
> *Venus*
> *Earth*
> *Mars*
> *Jupiter*
> *Saturn*
> *Uranus*
> *Neptune*

▶ The word terrestrial comes from the Latin word ___*terra*___ which means ___*earth*___.

▶ List the four terrestrial planets.

> *Mercury*
> *Venus*
> *Earth*
> *Mars*

▶ The term Jovian comes from ___*Jove, the god of the sky in Roman mythology*___

▶ List the four Jovian planets.

> *Jupiter*
> *Saturn*
> *Uranus*
> *Neptune*

Chapter 6: Our Solar System

Time Required

Text reading	30 minutes
Experimental	1 hour

Materials

the eight planet models from Experiment 5
ruler (in centimeters)
pencil
large flat surface for drawing—1 x 1 meter (3 x 3 feet), such as a
    large piece of cardboard or several sheets of construction paper
large open space at least 3 meters (10 feet) long
push pin
piece of string 1 meter (3 feet) long

Overall Objectives

This chapter takes a closer look at our solar system which is made up of the Sun and the eight planets orbiting it. Students will explore the inner and outer solar system, the distances of the planets from the Sun, and orbital paths and directions.

6.1 Introduction

This section introduces the term "solar system." Help the students understand that a solar system is a group of celestial bodies and the single sun they orbit. Our solar system has eight planets and includes an asteroid belt which is discussed in Section 6.4.

Explore open inquiry with the following questions:

- *Why do you think the Sun and the eight planets that orbit it are called a solar system?*

- *What do you think holds all the planets in their orbits around the Sun?*

- *Do you think other planets can join our solar system? Why or why not?*

- *How is the Sun different from the Moon and Earth?*

- *Do you think another Sun could join our solar system? Why or why not?*

6.2 Planetary Position

In this section students will learn about how the planets are ordered in the solar system. Recall from Chapter 1 that we now know that the Sun is the center of the solar system, and the Earth and the other seven planets orbit the Sun. Remind the students that this is called a heliocentric system. Recall that an Earth-centered system would be called geocentric.

Mercury is in orbit closest to the Sun, and Neptune is farthest from the Sun. Measuring planetary distances is challenging, especially because these distances are very great.

The units used in this text are astronomical units called AUs. The AU distances listed in the following table show planetary distances relative to the distance from the Earth to the Sun. In other words, the distance from the Earth to the Sun is 1 AU, and the other planetary distances are some fraction or multiple of 1 AU. Initially, planetary distances from the Sun were calculated using triangulation methods that required Earth's distance from the Sun as part of the calculation. This is why AUs are expressed as a fraction or multiple of Earth's distance from the Sun. However, with the use of radar, direct distances can now be calculated. (See *Experiment 2: Measuring Distances* for an example of the triangulation method.)

Planet	Distance from Sun (AUs)
Mercury	0.387
Venus	0.723
Earth	1.0
Mars	1.524
Jupiter	5.203
Saturn	9.554
Uranus	19.194
Neptune	30.066

Grasping long distances can be very difficult for students. In order for students to have a "feel" for how far AU distances are, the text relates the distance from the Earth to the Sun in terms of time—how long would it take to drive to the Sun going 97 kph (60 mph)? By understanding distance in this framework, students can more easily grasp these long distances.

Explore open inquiry with the following questions:

- *How easy or difficult do you think it is to measure the distance that Mercury is from the Earth?*

- *If scientists cannot use a tape measure or drive a car to Mars, how do we know how far it is?*

- *How accurate do you think the planetary distance measurements are?*

- *How important do you think it is to know math for calculating planetary distances?*

- *How long do you think it would take you to drive from the Earth to Jupiter going 97 kilometers per hour (60 miles per hour)?*

- *How long do you think it would take to drive from Earth to Neptune going 97 kilometers per hour (60 miles per hour)?*

- *Just for fun, how fast do you think you might have to go to get to Neptune in a few hours? Faster than a train? a boat? a jet? the speed of light?*

6.3 Planetary Orbits

In this section the students will explore the orbital paths of the planets. An orbit is defined as the curved path that a planet follows as it travels around the Sun.

Basic physics tells us that bodies of mass have gravity or gravitational force. The larger the body of mass, the more gravitational force it will have. The Sun is a very large body of mass and therefore has a very strong gravitational force. Gravity is what keeps the planets in orbit around the Sun.

The motion of the planets and the fact that the gravitational force of the Sun does not vary are what keep the planetary orbits from collapsing towards the center of the solar system.

Orbits are elliptical, but only slightly. A major misconception is that the elliptical orbit is what gives Earth the seasons. It is important that students understand that seasons are the result of the Earth tilting towards and away from the Sun, NOT the elliptical orbit. Earth's orbit and those of the planets are only slightly elliptical, so the distance from the Sun doesn't vary enough to cause seasons.

The solar system can be divided into two different groups of planets according to their distances from the Sun. These groups are called the inner solar system and the outer solar system, and there is a huge 4 AU gap between Mars (the outer planet of the inner solar system) and Jupiter (the inner planet of the outer solar system).

Explore open inquiry with the following questions:

- *Why do you think planetary orbits are mostly circular?*

- *Why don't the planets' orbits collapse towards the Sun? What keeps the planets orbiting?*

- *Do you think the gravitational force of the Sun extends beyond the solar system? Why or why not?*

- *Even though seasons are caused by the Earth's tilt and not how far the Earth is from the Sun, what do you think would happen to our seasons if the Earth's orbit were closer to the Sun? Farther from the Sun?*

6.4 Asteroids, Meteorites, and Comets

In this section students will look at a group of celestial bodies that orbit our Sun but are not planets. This group includes asteroids and comets. The gap between the inner and outer solar system is filled with millions of these smaller celestial bodies.

The terms used to describe the various celestial bodies can be a little confusing. Asteroids, meteors, and meteorites are three terms used to describe the same type of celestial body, but in different locations. Asteroids that enter Earth's atmosphere are called meteors, and if they impact the Earth, they are called meteorites. Asteroids are made of rock and minerals.

Comets are a different type of celestial body and are made of frozen carbon dioxide mixed with rocks and minerals. Comets do not appear to impact Earth as often as meteorites, and they are not given additional names.

6.5 Habitable Earth

In this section students explore the uniqueness of Earth in our solar system. Earth is the only celestial body known to support life, and it has many unique features that make life as we know it possible on this one planet in the solar system.

Explore open inquiry with the following questions:

- *Do you think life is possible on Mars? List all the reasons why or why not.*

- *Do you think life is possible on Jupiter? List all the reasons why or why not.*

- *Do you think there is enough energy from the Sun to support life on a moon orbiting Jupiter? Why or why not?*

- *Do you think liquid water can be found on Mercury? Why or why not?*

6.6 Summary

Go over the summary statements with the students and address any questions they might have.

- The terrestrial planets (Mercury, Venus, Earth, and Mars) make up the inner solar system and are "close" to the Sun (less than 2 AU).

- The Jovian planets (Jupiter, Saturn, Uranus, and Neptune) make up the outer solar system and are "far" from the Sun (more than 5 AU from the Sun).

- All of the eight planets have a slightly elliptical orbit (very close to circular).

- Asteroids exist throughout the solar system, but most asteroids are found in the Asteroid Belt between Mars and Jupiter.

- The Earth is the only known habitable celestial body in our solar system and is uniquely suited for life.

Help the students propose a possible objective. This is a model building experiment, so the students should focus their objective on what they will learn by building a model of the solar system.

The orbital path for Earth is set at 10 centimeters. This represents 1 AU from the Sun. The orbital distances will be circular in this model. Point out this difference to the students. Ask them how they might draw a more accurate orbital pathway.

Experiment 6: Modeling the Solar System Date: _____

Objective   *The objective of this experiment is to learn about relative planetary distances. (Example—answers may vary.)*

Hypothesis   *The model of the solar system will show the relative distances of the planets. (Example—answers may vary.)*

Materials

    the eight planet models from Experiment 5
    ruler (in centimeters)
    pencil
    large flat surface for drawing—1 x 1 meter (3 x 3 feet), such as a
       large piece of cardboard or several sheets of construction paper
    large open space at least 3 meters (10 feet) long
    push pin
    piece of string one meter (3 feet) long

Experiment

❶ In this experiment you will model the planetary orbits of the solar system.

❷ Take the cardboard and mark the center with a pen.

❸ Using the push pin, fix the string to the center mark of the cardboard.

❹ Wrap the free end of the string around the pencil. Position the pencil 10 centimeters from the center mark, pull the string tight, and with the pencil touching the cardboard, draw a circle around the center mark. This is the orbital path for Earth.

❺ Draw concentric circles for the first five planetary orbits (Mercury through Jupiter) using the distances listed below. You will need to adjust the length of the string for each orbit. Place the models of the planets you created in Experiment 5 at their corresponding orbit distance from the center.

Planet	Distance from Center
Mercury	4 cm
Venus	7 cm
Earth	10 cm
Mars	15 cm
Jupiter	50 cm
Saturn	90 cm (3 ft)
Uranus	190 cm (6 ft)
Neptune	300 cm (10 ft)

❻ For the last three orbits, walk to the correct distance away from the center. Place the planetary model you created in Experiment 5 at the appropriate distance.

Results

Observe your model of the solar system, and compare your model with the illustration on page 45 of your student textbook. On the following page, note any similarities or differences between your model of the solar system and the illustration.

The distances shown for the models of the planets are measured from the Sun (represented by the push pin at the center mark). Note that the first four orbits are relatively close together and that there is a 40 cm jump from Mars to Jupiter. *Optional:* Have the students draw the Asteroid Belt in this gap.

The orbital distances from the Sun for the last three planets are much greater than those for the inner planets. The relative distances in the experiment are based on the actual distances (note that Neptune is 30x farther from the Sun than Earth is). However, if your space is limited, you can have the students draw closer orbital paths for the outer three planets. Simply have the students make notes about any adjustments made to the spacing of the models and then discuss these adjustments in the Conclusions section.

Similarities	Differences

Conclusions

How easy or difficult was it to create a model of the solar system? How did the different distances affect how you could build your model?

_____

_____

_____

_____

_____

Review

Answer the following:

(Answers may vary.)

▶ The four terrestrial planets that make up the inner solar system are:

Mercury

Venus

Earth

Mars

▶ The four Jovian planets that make up the outer solar system are:

Jupiter

Saturn

Uranus

Neptune

▶ Define a planetary orbit.

the curved path of a planet around the Sun

▶ The orbits of the planets are nearly circular, but because they are not perfectly circular, they are called   *elliptical*

▶ The gap between the inner and outer planets is filled with

asteroids

▶ Why is Earth habitable but the other planets are not?

Earth has the right atmosphere, has liquid water, is the right distance

from the Sun, and has the Moon to stabilize it.

Chapter 7: Other Solar Systems

Time Required

Text reading	30 minutes
Experimental	1 hour

Materials

pen
paper
imagination

Overall Objectives

This chapter will explore other solar systems. Students will take a look at some of our nearest stars and the exoplanets that orbit these stars.

7.1 Introduction

The idea that there might be life on other planets comes from the overwhelming number of possible planets that could orbit the millions of stars in the universe. Because we know the criteria for life on Earth, astronomers can begin to look at stars and the planets that orbit those stars to determine if there are any planets that meet the criteria for life.

Explore open inquiry with the following questions:

- *Given what we know about Earth, what would a planet in another solar system need in order to support life?*

- *How easy or difficult is it for scientists to explore the possibility of life on other planets?*

- *How many other solar systems do you think exist?*

- *Do you think scientists have discovered all of the solar systems in the universe? Why or why not?*

- *Do you think other solar systems have the same number of planets as ours? Why or why not?*

7.2 Closest Stars

The three stars that are closest to our solar system are in the Alpha Centauri system. They are called Alpha Centauri A, Alpha Centauri B, and Proxima Centauri.

It is helpful for students to explore the interpretation of the map on page 52 of the student textbook. This diagram shows the positions of several of the stars that are closest to Earth. The concentric circles are in the same plane as the Sun. The straight lines show the approximate location of several stars relative to our Sun. Note that some stars are located above the plane of the Sun, and other stars are located below the plane.

Also, have the students notice that this illustration is a "qualitative" illustration, but because it does not note the distances between the concentric circles, it is not very "quantitative." Therefore, the illustration is useful for showing relative distances, but does not give any actual distances.

Explore open inquiry with the following questions:

- *Is the Alpha Centauri complex above or below the plane of concentric circles in the illustration?*
  (below)

- *Is the Alpha Centauri complex closer or farther from the Sun than Barnard's Star? How can you tell?*
  (The Alpha Centauri complex is closer because it is just below the first concentric circle, and Barnard's star is above the third concentric circle.)

- *Which star is closer: Wolf 359 or Lalande 21185?*
  (Lalande 21185)

7.3 Constellations

The students should already be familiar with some of the constellations from Chapter 1 and Experiment 1. It is important to notice that the constellations are groups of stars that seemingly form a particular pattern. However, the name of the constellation will vary from culture to culture. Also, the image on page 53 of the student textbook shows constellations for the northern hemisphere, but for students in the southern hemisphere, the constellations are different.

7.4 Brightest and Largest Stars

Star brightness is a measure of the energy that a star emits per unit area per unit time, and this depends on how far the star is from the observer. However, a star's luminosity (how much actual energy is released) is an intrinsic property of the star and does not depend on the star's distance from Earth. For example, when you turn on a flashlight, there is a certain amount of light energy being emitted. This is luminosity. However, if you were to stand 10 feet from the flashlight it would appear brighter than if you stood 50 feet away. This is brightness.

The apparent brightness of a star as viewed from Earth may not indicate how close it is to Earth relative to other stars. Stars with low luminosity (intrinsic energy) that are closer to Earth may appear less bright than stars with high luminosity that are farther away and appear brighter.

Astronomers use a magnitude scale to rank star brightness. Bright stars are ranked as first magnitude, with less bright stars having magnitudes of 2, 3, or higher. The brightness decreases as the magnitude value increases.

This section also introduces students to star sizes. Our Sun is a moderately sized star, and there are many stars that are magnitudes greater in brightness than the Sun.

Explore open inquiry with the following questions:

- *Why do you think Sirius, which is farther from Earth than Proxima Centauri, is the brightest star in the night sky?* (because it puts out more energy than Proxima Centauri)

- *What do you think Earth would be like if the Sun put out the same amount of energy as Sirius?*

- *What do you think Earth would be like if the Sun were as large as VY Canis Majoris?*

7.5 Planets Near Other Stars

Because the universe is home to millions of stars, it makes sense to assume that some of those stars have planets. The idea of the existence of other planets has fascinated both scientists and science fiction writers for many years, but the existence of exoplanets (planets in other solar systems) has only recently been confirmed.

Finding and studying exoplanets is extremely challenging. Because most exoplanets lie close to their parent star, direct imaging is difficult. An exoplanet can be observed by direct imaging if the parent star is weakly luminous or if the exoplanet makes a wide orbit.

However, exoplanets can be indirectly observed by analyzing light from the parent stars. Recall that planets have mass and because of this have a gravitational force. When a planet orbits a star, the star may "wobble" as a result of the planet's gravitational pull. The more massive the planet and the less massive the star, the more the star wobbles. Astronomers can use the wobbling of a star to estimate the mass of its exoplanets.

Explore open inquiry with the following questions:

- *Why do you think it is difficult to "see" exoplanets?*

- *How many exoplanets do you think might exist in the universe?*

- *What type of exoplanets do you think exist in other solar systems?*

- *Do you think there might be a type of exoplanet that is neither Jupiter-like nor Earth-like?*

7.6 The Circumstellar Habitable Zone

Although many exoplanets have been discovered, there are so far no exoplanets that seem to be suitable to support life as we know it. In order to support life, an exoplanet must be just the right distance from the parent star—neither too close nor too far away. This "Goldilocks distance" is called the Circumstellar Habitable Zone.

Explore open inquiry with the following questions:

- *What do you think would happen to life if Earth were closer to the Sun?*

- *What do you think would happen to life if Earth were farther from the Sun?*

- *If the Sun were twice as large and twice as hot, do you think the Earth would need to be closer to or farther from the Sun in order to be able to support life? Why or why not?*

- *If the Sun were half its size and half as hot, do you think the Earth would need to be closer or farther from the Sun in order to be able to support life? Why or why not?*

- *Do you think discovering whether an exoplanet is in a Circumstellar Habitable Zone is a useful criterion for determining if the planet can support life? Why or why not?*

7.7 Summary

Discuss the following summary statements with the students.

- Proxima Centauri in the Alpha Centauri system is our nearest stellar neighbor.

- The distances of stars are measured in parsecs. One parsec equals 206,260 AUs.

- Early astronomers grouped stars into patterns called constellations. Modern astronomers still use the names of constellations to discuss star positions.

- The stars that appear to be the brightest and largest are not the closest stars.

- Extrasolar planets (exoplanets) have been confirmed for many stars and billions more are estimated to exist.

- Earth is uniquely situated in an area called the Circumstellar Habitable Zone.

Experiment 7: Designing Life on Other Planets

Date: _____

Thought Experiment

Sometimes it's not possible to do an actual experiment, and yet it can be very useful to do what is called a "thought experiment." A thought experiment is a mental exercise in which an experiment is simply imagined. The process of imagining how a hypothesis might be explored or how an experiment might actually work is very valuable to science. Albert Einstein wondered what it would be like to ride on a rainbow. He could not literally ride on a rainbow, but he could imagine it, and the ideas he generated during this thought experiment helped him discover the theory of relativity.

Materials

pen
paper
your imagination

Experiment

❶   Imagine that you are traveling at the outer edges of our solar system and you come across a star three times the size of our Sun. You observe ten planets in the solar system around this sun. Some of the planets have moons. Assume that you can travel to all ten planets and explore all of their moons.

❷   Do a thought experiment and write in as much detail as possible what you would need to do to locate life on any of the ten planets or moons. Imagine this is really possible. Think about what you would need to take with you and how you would define "life." Also consider which planets are more likely to have life and which you can ignore.

This is a different type of experiment for students to explore. Thought experiments are very useful techniques for creative inquiry. In this experiment students will simply think about what life on other planets would require.

To help students begin to think about what life on an exoplanet might require, engage them with the following questions:

- *Would a planet that supports life need to be a Jupiter-like or Earth-like planet? Why or why not?*

- *Would a planet that supports life need liquid water? Why or why not?*

- *What would be required for a planet to have liquid water? (an atmosphere, stable temperatures between 0 and 100 degrees C, stable pressures, etc.)*

- *How far from the parent star would a planet need to be? (close enough for adequate energy [heat] but not too close, etc.)*

- *How about the chemistry of life on your planet? Is it carbon-based? Silicon-based? Or based on metals?*

- *If metal-based life is possible, could the exoplanet be closer or farther from the parent star? Why or why not?*

  ...and so on.

The questions that can be asked are endless and the objective is to have fun exploring all the possibilities for life on an exoplanet. By imagining what life could look like on an exoplanet, students will gain a deeper understanding of why life is possible on Earth.

Have the students write as many details as possible about what life might look like on an exoplanet. Encourage them to use their imagination.

Finding Life

_____

_____

_____

_____

_____

_____

_____

_____

_____

_____

_____

_____

_____

_____

_____

_____

_____

_____

_____

_____

_____

_____

_____

_____

_____

_____

_____

_____

_____

_____

_____

_____

_____

_____

_____

_____

_____

Review

Answer the following:

(Answers may vary.)

▶ The three stars that are closest to our solar system are part of a triple-star system called the ___Alpha Centauri system___.

The three stars in this system are:

___Proxima Centauri___

___Alpha Centauri A___

___Alpha Centauri B___

▶ A parsec is ___206,260___ AUs.

▶ The brightest star in the sky is called ___Sirius___.

▶ The largest star in the sky is called ___VY Canis Majoris___.

▶ An exoplanet is a planet that:

___orbits a star outside our solar system___

___

___

▶ Define the Circumstellar Habitable Zone.

___the optimal distance between a planet and its parent star that would___

___enable the planet to support life___

___

___

Chapter 8: Our Galaxy

Time Required

Text reading	30 minutes
Experimental	1 hour

Materials

pen
paper
computer and internet service
Google Earth

Overall Objectives

In this chapter students begin to explore the space beyond our solar system by learning about the Milky Way Galaxy which contains our solar system along with other solar systems and stars. Students will examine in detail the galaxy that is our home.

8.1 Introduction

In the last chapter students explored the stars and planets that make up other solar systems. Now they will see that despite the fact that the spaces between stars and solar systems are very large, stars and solar systems exist in organized groups called galaxies.

Explore open inquiry with the following questions:

- *In the last several chapters you learned that the planets that orbit our Sun are organized into a solar system and that there are other stars and planets organized into other solar systems. Do you think the solar systems that are near us are organized into some specific pattern or shape? Why or why not?*

- *If other solar systems were organized into a group that included ours, do you think our Sun would be at the center of this group? Why or why not?*

- *If you were to organize our neighboring solar systems, how might you do it? Would you spread them out, bunch them together, or do a little of both?*

- *Do you think there is any reason why solar systems might be organized?*

8.2 The Milky Way

In this section students discover that stars and planets are not just randomly distributed in space but organized into very large clusters called galaxies. Galaxies form because stars and planets have gravity, and gravitational forces hold solar systems and galaxies together. Our Sun and solar system reside in the galaxy called The Milky Way.

Gathering information about our galaxy is difficult, mainly because we live inside of it. A useful analogy is to compare mapping our galaxy to a scuba diver trying to map the entire ocean. A scuba diver can map only a small area because he can see only a small area. However, if the scuba diver could fly in a plane, he would be able to get more information about the ocean. In other words, it would be easier to study the whole ocean if the scuba diver could take himself out of the ocean to gain a wider view.

We cannot take ourselves out of our galaxy to get a wider view of it, so the best way to learn about our own galaxy is by exploring other galaxies. Students will learn about other galaxies in Chapter 9.

The first astronomer who attempted to map our galaxy was William Herschel, and he assumed that the Milky Way Galaxy was a flat, disk-shaped cluster with our Sun in the center. Today we know that Herschel's estimation was incorrect.

To get an idea of how difficult it is to map a large area, have your students explore the following exercise.

- *Sit in the middle of a room, and using the information you can see with your eyes, draw a map of what you see in the room.*

- *Still sitting in the middle of the room, map the rest of the building.*

- *Continue sitting in the middle of the room, and map the nearby neighborhood.*

- *Bring your map farther out, and map the city you live in.*

- *Finally, still sitting in the middle of the room, map the state and then the country you live in.*

Explore open inquiry with the following questions:

- *How easy or difficult is it to map an area you cannot directly investigate?*

- *How accurate is the map of your room, building, neighborhood, city, state, or country?*

- *What would help you create a more accurate map of your room, building, neighborhood, city, state, or country?*

8.3 Shape and Size

We have never observed our entire galaxy directly, but based on observations of other galaxies, astronomers have concluded that The Milky Way is a spiral galaxy with a bulge in the center and thin and thick disks extending outwards. Our solar system is located on one of the small, partial spiral arms in the thin disk area of the Milky Way Galaxy.

Since Earth is located outside the galactic bulge, we "see" the Milky Way Galaxy as a thick band of stars in the night sky. When we see this band of stars, we are looking directly into the galactic disk of the Milky Way. When we look perpendicular to this thick band of stars, we are no longer looking into the galactic disk, and we no longer see the Milky Way.

Calculating the size of the Milky Way Galaxy is very difficult for astronomers. Again, it would be like trying to make a map of an entire city while remaining in one place. Because of this, astronomers' conclusions about the size of the Milky Way Galaxy are ambiguous and inconclusive.

Explore open inquiry with the following questions:

- *Do you think astronomers' ideas about the size and shape of the Milky Way Galaxy are accurate? Why or why not?*

- *If Earth were located in the center of the Milky Way Galaxy, would it be easier to measure the size of the Milky Way Galaxy? Why or why not?*

- *Do you think galaxies would exist if planets and stars had no gravity? Why or why not?*

8.4 Galactic Habitable Zone

A curious observation is that our planet resides in the particular section of the Milky Way Galaxy that makes life on Earth possible. Just as the Circumstellar Habitable Zone is the area of optimal distance between planets and their parent star where life might be possible, so also is the galactic habitable zone the optimal distance and location for a solar system in a galaxy to have the right conditions for life, being neither too far away nor too close to the center of the galaxy. The galactic habitable zone can be used as one criterion for examining solar systems and their exoplanets to determine if life is possible on those planets.

8.5 Summary

Discuss the following summary statements with the students.

- A galaxy is a large collection of stars, gas, dust, planets, and other objects held together by its own gravity.

- The Milky Way Galaxy is a spiral shaped galaxy with a central bulge at the center of a thin disk.

- The size of the Milky Way Galaxy is estimated to be 30 kiloparsecs (kpc).

- Earth resides between the Sagittarius and Perseus arms on a small, partial spiral arm called the Orion Arm.

- Our solar system is uniquely situated in an area called the galactic habitable zone which provides conditions necessary for life as we know it to exist.

This experiment gives students a chance to use and evaluate data. The data in the table found in the Appendix at the back of the Laboratory Workbook has already been sorted for the students, and the only column they need to examine is the *Constellation* column (*Con*). The objective of this experiment is to use data that shows the number of globular clusters in a constellation. Since the densest group of stars is at the center of the Milky Way Galaxy, those constellations with the largest number of globular clusters are found at the center of the galaxy. Students need to use Google Earth for this experiment. A short setup process for Google Earth is given.

Help the students write a valid objective and hypothesis. Answers may vary.

Experiment 8: The Center of the Milky Way   Date: _____

Objective   *To use data tables in order to find the center of the Milky Way Galaxy*

Hypothesis   *The center of the Milky Way Galaxy will be found near the constellations with the highest number of globular clusters.*

Materials

pen
paper
computer and internet service
Google Earth

Experiment

❶ Set up Google Earth on your computer.

① Go to http://earth.google.com and click "Download Google Earth."

② Click "Agree and Download."

③ Once the file has been downloaded, install the program.

④ Open the Google Earth program on your computer.

⑤ Set up Google Earth in Sky Mode.

⑥ At the top, click "View" and then click "Switch to Sky."

⑦ On the left-hand side of the window, you should see "Layers."

⑧ Uncheck every item except "Imagery" and "Backyard Astronomy."

⑨ Click the arrow next to "Backyard Astronomy."

⑩ Uncheck every item except "Constellations."

❷ The *Appendix* at the back of this book gives data for globular clusters observed in our Milky Way Galaxy. The data table shows 158 globular clusters compiled as of June 30, 2010. From left to right the table lists the ID, name, and cross-reference for the cluster followed by the constellation where the cluster is located and various astronomical parameters associated with the cluster.

❸ Look at the data table in the *Appendix*, and locate the three constellations that have the highest number of globular clusters. [Note: The number of globular clusters observed in a constellation is found in parentheses next to the constellation name. Constellations with fewer than two globular clusters are not listed.]

❹ Write the three constellations with the highest number of globular clusters below.

Constellation Name	# of Globular Clusters

Results

❶ Open Google Earth and toggle the "sky" button so that you are looking at the sky. In the "Search the Sky" button, type in the name of one of the three constellations you listed above. Adjust the view so that you see all three constellations. This location should be the center of the Milky Way Galaxy.

❷ Type in "galactic center" to check your results.

Conclusions

Based on your observations, where is the galactic center of the Milky Way? How easy or difficult do you think it is to find the center of a galaxy?

_____

_____

_____

_____

_____

_____

_____

_____

_____

_____

_____

_____

_____

_____

_____

_____

Review

Answer the following:
(Answers may vary.)

▶ Write a definition of galaxy.

  a gigantic collection of stars, planets, and other celestial bodies

  grouped together

▶ What are the three basic categories of galaxies?

  spirals

  ellipticals

  irregulars

▶ What type of galaxy is the Milky Way?   *spiral*

▶ List the names of the two major spiral arms and two minor spiral arms of the Milky Way Galaxy.

  Scutum-Centaurus (major)   *Norma Arm (minor)*

  Perseus (major)   *Sagittarius Arm (minor)*

▶ Define the galactic habitable zone.

  the space in a galaxy that is most suitable for life

Chapter 9: Other Galaxies

Time Required

Text reading   30 minutes
Experimental   1 hour

Materials

pen
paper
computer and internet service
Google Earth

Overall Objectives

In this chapter students begin to explore other galaxies. Our Milky Way Galaxy is just one of billions of galaxies in the universe. In Chapter 8 students were introduced to three different types of galaxies, and now students will examine a few types of galaxies in more detail.

9.1 Introduction

In this chapter students will look at galaxies outside the Milky Way. Students have learned that the Milky Way is a spiral galaxy with several arms and a bulging galactic center that is dense with stars. But not all galaxies are shaped like ours.

Classifying galaxies can be challenging because of their variety. However, the Hubble classification system that was introduced by Edwin Hubble in 1936 is still used today.

Explore open inquiry with the following questions.

- *Besides a spiral galaxy like the Milky Way, what other galaxy shapes might exist?*

- *Do you think all spiral galaxies are the same? Why or why not?*

- *How many galaxies do you think exist in the universe?*

- *Do you think we have discovered all possible galaxy types? Why or why not?*

- *How would you go about classifying a galaxy?*

9.2 Spiral Galaxies

Students explored our own spiral galaxy in Chapter 8. In this section students will take a closer look at several other spiral galaxies.

All spiral galaxies have spiral arms extending from a bulging galactic center and forming a flattened disk.

The Andromeda Galaxy is our nearest spiral neighbor. Notice that the galaxy has several different names and is an Sb galaxy, meaning that it is a medium sized spiral galaxy.

Messier 81, or M81, is another spiral galaxy and is tilted with respect to ours. This tilt enables us to easily visualize this galaxy.

Other spiral galaxies to explore are NGC 3344, the "Hubble Backward Spiral" NGC 4622, and NGC 300. Images for these galaxies can be found at http://www.nasaimages.org or by using Google Earth.

Explore open inquiry with the following questions.

- *Why do you think some galaxies form a spiral that has extended arms?*
(from gravitational forces)

- *If you were to look for life in the Andromeda Galaxy where would you look first?*
(in the galactic habitable zone)

- *If M81 were not tilted, do you think we could easily see its arms? Why or why not?*

9.3 Barred Spiral Galaxies

A barred spiral galaxy is a galaxy with the spiral arms extending from an elongated region, or "bar," in the galactic bulge. Many astronomers believe that the Milky Way may be a barred spiral galaxy. However, barred spiral galaxies can be difficult to distinguish from spiral galaxies.

Other barred spiral galaxies to explore are NGC 1672 and NGC 4319. Images for these galaxies can be found at http://www.nasaimages.org or by using Google Earth.

9.4 Elliptical Galaxies

Elliptical galaxies have no discernible arms, bars, or internal features. These galaxies are more uniform in shape with an increase of stellar material towards the center.

Other elliptical galaxies to explore are the large elliptical galaxy ESO 325-G004, the galaxy NGC-1132, and HCG-87b (in the Hickson Compact Group 87). Images for these galaxies can be found at http://www.nasaimages.org or by using Google Earth.

9.5 Irregular Galaxies

Galaxies that don't fit into any of the other categories are called irregular galaxies.

Some irregular galaxies to explore are NGC 265, Starburst Galaxy M82, and NGC 1427A. Images for these galaxies can be found at http://www.nasaimages.org or by using Google Earth.

9.6 Summary

Discuss the following summary questions with the students:

- Hubble's classification scheme divides galaxies into four major groups: 1) spiral, 2) barred spiral, 3) elliptical, and 4) irregular.

- Spiral and barred spiral galaxies both have spiral arms extending from a galactic bulge. In the case of barred spiral galaxies, the galactic bulge is elongated.

- Elliptical galaxies are either circular or elongated.

- Irregular galaxies have no defined shape.

Experiment 9: Finding Galaxies
Date: _____

Objective
To explore different galaxies using Google Earth (Answers may vary.)

Hypothesis
Galaxies can be observed and categorized using Hubble's categories. (Answers may vary.)

Materials

pen
paper
computer and internet service
Google Earth

Experiment

❶ Open the Google Earth program on your computer.

(If you have not yet set up Google Earth on your computer, see the instructions in Experiment 8.)

① At the top, click "View" and then click "Switch to Sky," or click on the planet symbol.

② On the left-hand side of the window, you should see "Layers."

③ Uncheck every item, except "Imagery" and "Backyard Astronomy."

④ Click the arrow next to "Backyard Astronomy."

⑤ Uncheck every item except "Constellations."

❷ Using Google Earth, do a search for the galaxies listed in the following table. Categorize each galaxy as either spiral, elliptical, or irregular

Name	Type
Whirlpool Galaxy	*spiral*
NGC 1427A	*irregular*
M 101	*spiral or barred spiral*
M 82	*irregular*
Bode's Galaxy	*spiral*
M 87	*elliptical*
Sombrero Galaxy	*spiral*
Sunflower Galaxy	*spiral*
Hoag's Object	*spiral or irregular*
Cartwheel Galaxy	*irregular*
NGC 3314	*spiral*

Results

❶ Look for two galaxies that are not named.

❷ Draw each below, give the location, assign a name, and list the type.

location

name

type

location

name

type

Have the students peruse space using Google Earth. Suggested galaxies are:

Messier 79 (M79)
irregular; near Lepus constellation

Messier 55 (M55)
irregular; Sagittarius constellation

Messier 69 (M69)
irregular; Sagittarius constellation

Conclusions

Based on your observations, how easy or difficult is it to identify galaxies and categorize them? What else did you discover about galaxies?

_____

_____

_____

_____

_____

_____

_____

_____

_____

_____

_____

_____

_____

_____

_____

_____

Review

(Answers may vary.)

Answer the following:

▶ What is the name and type of our closest galactic neighbor?

Andromeda Galaxy

spiral

▶ What is the difference between a barred spiral galaxy and a spiral galaxy? Draw each below.

A barred spiral galaxy has spiral arms extending from a bar in the

middle. A spiral galaxy has spiral arms extending from the galactic

bulge.

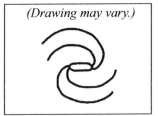
(Drawing may vary.)

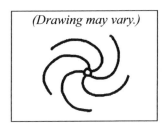
(Drawing may vary.)

▶ What is the difference between elliptical galaxies and irregular galaxies?

Elliptical galaxies are ellipse-shaped, have no spiral arms or galactic

bulge, and have more stars toward the center. Irregular galaxies have

no discernible shape and don't fit into any other categories.

Chapter 10: The Universe

Time Required

Text reading	30 minutes
Experimental	1 hour

Materials

pen
paper
computer and internet service
Google Earth

Overall Objectives

In this chapter students take a look at celestial bodies and other features of the universe that have not been covered so far. By this time the students should see how Earth sits in a solar system and how our solar system sits in a galaxy and how our galaxy sits among billions of other galaxies in the universe.

10.1 Introduction

In the last chapter students explored a variety of different galactic shapes and sizes. All of these galaxies exist in the space we call the universe. In this chapter students will begin to explore other features of the universe that have not yet been covered.

Explore open inquiry with the following questions.

- *You have studied planets, stars, solar systems, and galaxies. What else might be in the universe?*

- *Do you think the universe is static (remaining constant) or dynamic (changing over time)? Why or why not?*

- *How big do you think the universe is?*

- *Do you think the universe is infinite and has no end? Or do you think the universe is finite and, although very large, ends?*

- *If the universe is finite, what do you think lies outside of it?*

10.2 Red Giants and White Dwarfs

Stars change over time. Although the energy produced by our Sun will remain constant for a very long time to come, its hydrogen will eventually run out, and the Sun will no longer have any fuel for the thermonuclear reactions that produce light and heat energy.

It appears that stars begin, grow, and die. During this process stars go through a number of changes. Scientists believe that when our Sun began, it was larger and hotter than it is today, and when it has used up all its hydrogen, it will eventually expand into a red giant. Eventually, the Sun will burn out, becoming a white dwarf. Although no astronomer has actually seen the progression from birth to death of a single star, by observing stars at different stages, scientists can predict what will happen to a star as it changes over time.

Explore open inquiry with the following questions.

- *What do you think will happen to Earth when our Sun becomes a red giant?*

- *Do you think life on a planet could survive the type of changes its star would undergo while turning into a red giant or white dwarf?*

- *Do you think all stars go through the same changes? Why or why not?*

10.3 Novae and Supernovae

Although novae and supernovae are both stars that suddenly increase in brightness, they are different types of stellar phenomena.

A nova is an old star that has used up its own hydrogen and now captures hydrogen from a nearby star to use as a fuel source. As a result, a nova will cycle between periods of high and then low luminosity as it acquires and then burns up hydrogen.

A supernova, on the other hand, is a star that is exploding. A star that becomes a supernova will increase in luminosity until it explodes, and then it will gradually fade away, leaving stellar debris behind.

Explore open inquiry with the following questions.

- *If our Sun started to become a supernova, how might life on Earth change?*

- *If our Sun became a nova, how might life on Earth change?*

- *A nova can take hydrogen from neighboring stars. Do you think there are stars close enough to our Sun from which it could take hydrogen as fuel? Why or why not?*

10.4 Black Holes and Nebulae

Astronomers think that a black hole is a type of stellar debris. It is believed that a black hole begins as a supernova whose core collapses due to the effects of gravity. This causes the electrons and protons in the supernova's core to combine to form neutrons, resulting in an extremely dense neutron star. The further collapse of this neutron star then results in a black hole being formed. Because a black hole's gravitational pull is so strong, no form of radiation, including x-rays, visible light rays, and radio waves, can escape the black hole.

For this reason, black holes cannot be directly observed but are inferred by the "lack of information" available and by their effect on other matter.

Nebulae are another type of stellar debris. Nebulae are clouds of dust, hydrogen, helium, ionized matter, and other gases. Nebulae form some of the most beautiful galactic features in the universe.

10.5 A Universe We Can Discover

It is a fascinating fact that the universe is discoverable by humans not only because humans have developed the technology to explore space, but also because Earth is situated at just the right place in the solar system, with just the right atmosphere, and in just the right place in the galaxy to make exploring the universe possible.

> Explore open inquiry with the following questions.
>
> - *Would we be able to study the universe if a black hole were in our solar system? Why or why not?*
>
> - *Would we be able to study the universe if we lived on Jupiter? Why or why not?*
>
> - *How might our study of the universe change if Earth were located in the middle of a nebula?*

10.6 Summary

Discuss the following summary points with the students:

- A red giant is a star that has become larger, brighter, and hotter as it begins to burn helium for fuel.

- A white dwarf is a star that has used up all of its own fuel, leaving just the core.

- Novae are stars that increase in luminosity, fade, and then become bright again.

- A supernova is a star that suddenly increases in luminosity as it explodes, and then it slowly fades.

- A black hole is believed to occur when a large amount of mass from a stellar remnant occupies a small amount of space.

- Nebulae are clouds of dust, gases, and ionized matter.

Experiment 10: Searching for Nebulae   Date: _____

Objective   *To explore various nebulae using Google Earth*

(Answers may vary.)

Hypothesis   *More nebulae are going to be located near the center of the*

Milky Way. (Answers may vary.)

Materials

  pen
  paper
  computer and internet service
  Google Earth

Experiment

❶ Open the Google Earth program on your computer.

(If you have not yet set up Google Earth on your computer, see the instructions in Experiment 8.)

① At the top, click "View," and then click "Switch to Sky."

② On the left-hand side of the window, you should see "Layers."

③ Uncheck every item, except "Imagery" and "Backyard Astronomy."

④ Click the arrow next to "Backyard Astronomy."

⑤ Uncheck every item except "Constellations."

❷ Using Google Earth, search for the following nebulae. Illustrate what you observe, and note the location of each nebula by naming any nearby constellations.

(Drawings and answers may vary.)

Helix Nebula

location
_____
_____

Cat's Eye Nebula

location
_____
_____

Crab Nebula

location
_____
_____

Eagle Nebula

location
_____
_____

Cone Nebula

location
_____
_____

Orion Nebula

location
_____
_____

All of the nebulae can be found by typing the exact name into Google Earth. The cursor will point to the nebula. You can zoom in or out to find the nearby constellations.

Helix Nebula
located between Aquarius, Capricornus, and Piscis Austrinus

Cat's Eye Nebula
near Draco

Crab Nebula
between Auriga, Gemini, Orion, and Taurus

Eagle Nebula
near Serpens Cauda

Cone Nebula
between Gemini, Canis Minor, Orion, and Monoceres

Orion Nebula
in Orion constellation

Have the students "play" with Google Earth, noticing and recording any interesting galactic features. There are no right or wrong answers and results will vary.

❸ Using Google Earth, scan the sky by moving the window left and right, up and down, zooming in and zooming out.

❹ Search for a black hole. Draw what you observe. Also search for any other objects you find interesting, and label them star, galaxy, nebula, or black hole.

location _____ _____ type _____ _____	location _____ _____ type _____ _____
location _____ _____ type _____ _____	location _____ _____ type _____ _____

Results

Describe what you discovered.

_____

_____

_____

_____

_____

Conclusions

How easy or difficult is it to identify nebulae or other features in the sky? Do you think all of the galaxies, stars, and nebulae in the universe have been discovered? Why or why not?

_____

_____

_____

_____

_____

_____

_____

_____

_____

_____

_____

_____

_____

_____

_____

Have the students draw conclusions based on their observations. Discuss with students why it is unlikely that all of the galaxies, stars, and nebulae have been discovered.

Review

(Answers may vary.)

Answer the following:

1. What is a red giant star?

   a star that has begun to fuse helium, causing its thermonuclear reactions

   to increase to the point that the star expands, creating more heat and light

2. What is a white dwarf star?

   a star that has used all of its fuel

3. What happens to a star that has become a nova or supernova?

   a nova is a white dwarf that cycles between high and low luminosity by

   acquiring hydrogen fuel from a neighboring star

   a supernova is an exploding star

4. Knowing that the center of the Milky Way Galaxy is full of stars, do you think that when you are looking for objects in the sky, such as nebulae, it is an advantage that Earth is located on an outside spiral arm of the galaxy? Why or why not?

   answers will vary

Made in the USA
San Bernardino, CA
15 January 2017